C 3/16

Convoys and the U-bo

by John Gallehawk

CONTENTS

The Author
John Gallehawk B.Sc is a statistician
and a volunteer with the Bletchley Park Trust
© 1997 John Gallehawk

Convoys and the U-boats

The title of this booklet is "Convoys and the U-boats". You will notice the use of the plural. It would require great temerity even to contemplate covering this topic in a single booklet. Several volumes would be nearer the mark.

This account is thus restricted to a period in early 1943. The events describe three convoys and involvement with the many U-boats – there must have been many of our fellow countrymen at the time who would fervently have preferred were it not so.

To set the scene I shall describe the U-boat development and then move to the awesome events of the convoys.

The U-boat fleet at the outbreak of war

Several senior German naval officers, in outlining the development of the fleet before the war, stated that an outbreak of hostilities with Great Britain had been considered unlikely, and the fleet had been planned on this understanding. The original plan envisaged a small, well-balanced fleet capable of a useful but subsidiary role in a war against another continental power, but incapable of playing any part in a war against a major sea power.

For this reason, Germany readily accepted the terms of the Anglo-German Naval Treaty of 1935, which permitted her to build submarines up to fifty per cent of the number in the British fleet.

Although Germany did not build the full number allowed, even this would not have given her a fleet of U-boats comparable to that possessed in the 1914-1918 war.

Had Great Britain been considered as a potential enemy, taking into consideration the short time they might expect to have at their disposal, the Germans would have planned a fleet with a far higher proportion of U-boats. They could not hope to build a surface fleet capable of challenging the British in less than ten years, but a fleet of about two hundred U-boats might have been possible within five years if no provision for capital ships had been made.

A truer way of stating the case would be that in planning the new fleet in the early days of the Nazi regime, the German High Command had no specific enemy in mind, but was merely concerned to create a representative naval force sufficient to sustain the dignity of the new Germany.

At the outbreak of war Germany found herself with a U-boat fleet which was quite inadequate both in types and numbers for the tasks it had to face. The German officers blamed the politicians for not directing policy to ensure peace with Great Britain or else that an adequate U-boat fleet was ready, or planned, in case of hostilities.

Nearly half the total number of U-boats completed before the war were small Type II boats of 250 to 300 tons, their range limited to no further than the English Channel.

The Type lld had a saddle tank which gave it an endurance of 5,650 miles at 8 knots, which allowed Atlantic patrols of four weeks duration.

After the Munich crisis of 1938 the building policy shifted to medium U-boats, this accelerated when Germany began to consider the probability of war with Great Britain. *See Table 1 U-boat statistics.*

The Type Vllc was the most important of the U-boat types comprising 58% of boats built between 1935 and the end of 1944. It was the normal 500 ton fighting boat with which the German navy fought the anti-commerce war during the critical period 1941 to 1943. Only four were commissioned before the war.

The first boat of the larger 740 ton Type lX left the slips in 1938 and 8 were operational by the end of 1939. The Type lXc was to become the most common fighting boat after the Vllc. A total of 141 were built by two yards during the war. Three yards were engaged on the construction of U-boats by 1939, two at Kiel and one at Bremen.

By September 1939, of sixty completed boats, 35 were ready for active service and 8 others nearly so. Half of this small force consisted of short-range Type II craft incapable of operating in the western approaches to the British Isles, which was the focal point of submarine warfare aimed at the blockade of Britain.

In August 1939, Admiral Dönitz assumed less than half of the fleet to be operationally effective at any given moment and estimated a minimum of 300 U-boats for decisive operations.

After the end of the war he claimed, that a realistic policy would have a fleet of 1,000 U-boats at the beginning of hostilities. The difference between either estimate and the number actually available at the outbreak of hostilities, is a measure of Germany's failure to provide for the situation that resulted from her political strategy.

In October 1939, U-boats were given the highest priority by Grossadmiral Raeder the Commander-in-Chief of the navy, orders were placed for a vastly increased construction programme in thirteen yards in addition to the original three.

It was calculated that a construction period of about twenty-one months must be envisaged for U-boats laid down in September 1939, with a further three months for working-up and training before such boats became operational. So that the measures taken could not affect the situation at sea for nearly two years.

In the meantime, the operational fleet, commissioned or laid down before the war, would fall far short of requirements. This led to negotiations for the purchase of submarines with Japan, Italy and Russia. None were successful, and until the collapse of France and the occupation of certain other European countries no foreign submarines were added to the U-boat arm. The total number appropriated is not known, but approximately ten were commissioned by the Germans, mostly for training purposes.

The distance of German bases from the Atlantic encouraged the refuelling of U-boats at sea, to increase the operational time.

The superior strength of the Royal Navy made it unlikely that refuelling activities could be carried out with surface tankers. The alternative was to build large U-boats designed to fulfil this function. The amount of fuel handed over to a 500 ton fighting boat at sea would increase its operational endurance by three weeks.

The original series of six Type XIV boats was completed by the spring of 1942. A further final set of four boats, also built by Deutsche Werke Kiel, were completed during the winter of 1942-1943.

The reason for the failure to implement the original programme of eighteen boats is not known, but possibly increasing shortages made the Germans reluctant to spend the necessary labour and materials on the construction of such large and expensive boats.

Designed for refuelling other boats as their main object, the armament of the U-tankers was purely defensive and no torpedo-tubes were fitted, high fuel capacity was the main consideration. The bulk of the 740 cubic metres of heavy diesel oil carried was available to replenish other boats.

Between 30 to 40 cubic metres was normally handed over to each fighting boat at refuelling although some boats received only 5 to 10 cubic metres to enable them to return to port. A large number of boats were thus served in a single tanker cruise.

The refuelling operation was carried out on the surface by a hose suspended on floats attached to a wire rope. The hazardous operation was only attempted in isolated areas of the Atlantic in an attempt to avoid allied aircraft activity. The rate of fuel transfer was about 25 cubic metres an hour and so lasted for up to 2 hours on each boat.

Sources Of Intelligence

On 14th September 1939, U-39 fell victim to HM ships Faulkner, Foxhound and Firedrake. The results of prisoner interrogations were issued as a confidential book. This began a series of publications throughout the war that contributed much to the Allies' knowledge of the construction and disposition of the German U-boat fleet. By the end of the war approximately 5,000 prisoners had been taken from 181 U-boats. While there was much conflicting evidence from this source, it did provide valuable insight into aspects of the U-boat war that would otherwise have remained a closed book as far as intelligence was concerned.

Photographic reconnaissance and agent reports provided information but special intelligence contributed little on building policy or the disposition of forces between various areas, nor was there much by way of discussion of the various types and performance of U-boats. On the other hand, a detailed study of signals, particularly from the Baltic over a lengthy period, threw considerable light on such matters, above all on the number of commissioned U-boats.

Baltic security regulations required boats to report by W/T when passing the barrage at Gedser and as all newly commissioned boats from Keil and North Sea yards passed the barrage on their way to the training areas, early knowledge of their existence was available, so that the average delay between commissioning and the first reference to it in Special Intelligence was about one month.

It was frequently possible to identify the Type of an operational U-boat by fuel report analysis, particularly so after the capture and subsequent Royal Navy sea-trials of U-570 in 1941, which provided useful data on 500-ton boat fuel consumption.

U-boats were built as a series by the various yards and numbered consecutively; Type determination of one of the series identified the rest. Occasionally the type was identified by flotilla membership.

The Development of the U-boat Fleet

By 1944 attempts had been made to identify the Type and building yard of every boat mentioned in Special Intelligence. Captured documents confirmed or corrected these identifications and by Christmas it was possible to publish a complete survey of the U-boat construction schedule.

Chart 1 is a graph of the results of the U-boat building policy throughout the war in terms of tonnage and numbers.

It is interesting to compare this with the number of net additions to the Operational Fleet in Chart 2. If all boats were sent on active service as soon as their working-up and pre-operational training were finished, the size of the operational fleet would depend on the rate of production on one hand and the rate of losses on the other. Chart 2 shows this net result. During the first 18 months of the war, (see 1939-40) the output of boats was insufficient to compensate for losses with the consequence of a net reduction in the size of the fleet in this period.

The actual figures can be seen in Chart 3, which shows the Operational Fleet at just over 40 boats in September 1939 falling to under 25 by the beginning of 1941. The first 18 months is prior to the effects from the programme, laid down after the outbreak of war, had begun to take effect. Additions to the fleet were those boats laid down before September 1939.

The effectiveness of the U-boat fleet in these early days was limited by size and the type of craft in the fleet. Well over half the active service boats were confined by endurance to North Sea operations, not an area of great significance in a commerce war against Britain, whose important trade routes were across the Atlantic.

The small Type ll and the original Type Vll boats were allocated to the North Sea and the east coast of the United Kingdom. The improved Type Vllb and Vllc were sent to the Western Approaches while the few Type lX boats available were employed in more distant areas, such as the approaches to Gibraltar.

Before the acquisition of bases in western France and the commissioning of U-tankers, the problem of achieving the maximum operational time for each U-boat was solved by the use of surface supply ships stationed at sea and German merchant ships lying in the ports of El Ferrol, Vigo and Cadiz in Spain and Las Palmas in the Canaries.

Using the Dover Straits to shorten the passage time to areas west of the United Kingdom caused the loss of several boats, mainly by mines and the practice was abandoned by the end of 1939.

Chart 4, shows the monthly averages for boats on operations, together with losses. These averages, even if inaccurate, were constructed by the Germans and used as the basis for their policy. It can be seen that the average number of boats on operations from the beginning of the war to the end of 1940 was well below 20 – the average for the whole period is the pitifully small number of 14. Percentage losses declined from about 20% to about 10% by the end of the period.

On the other hand, the achievements of this force were considerable in relation to numbers. In the days when the British anti-submarine effort was only beginning, the Germans exploited the possibility of operating close to the shores of the United Kingdom. Although there could be no question of saturating the defence, a small number of U-boats stood a high chance of success in these coastal waters where shipping routes converged.

Expansion to the Atlantic

By the spring of 1941, British defences around the United Kingdom made it extremely dangerous for U-boats, and the command was obliged to shift to the open Atlantic. This increased the proportion of each cruise spent on passage to the operational area.

Two factors tended to counteract this disadvantage. First, the effects of the building programme laid down in the last months of 1939 began to show the greater flow of new boats to the operational fleet. Chart 1 shows the steep rise in the number of newly commissioned boats from mid 1940. Allowing about three to four months' working-up time in the Baltic, the rise begins to affect the operational fleet in the 2nd quarter of 1941. Chart 2 shows this change when additions to the Operational Fleet overtake losses for the first time.

Secondly, completion of U-boat bases on the Atlantic coast of France gave a reduction in time spent on passage. This more than compensated for the shift of activity to the open Atlantic. As a result, the monthly average of boats on operations rose from 8 boats in December 1940 to just under 40 by the autumn of 1941. Percentage loss of boats on operations remained slightly over 10% until mid 1942 after which it declined further.

In September 1941, U-boats operated as a separate command for the first time in northern waters from ports in northern Norway. By the summer of 1942, a force of 23 boats were in the area. Although operational needs of other areas caused the total to reduce to 12 in October 1943, it reached a peak of 33 by May 1944. The proximity of the bases in northern Norway enabled the smaller 500-ton U-boats to be employed against Allied convoys to Russia.

The establishment of a force of 500-ton U-boats in the Mediterranean began about the same time as the expansion to northern waters, *U-97*, the ill-fated *U-559* and *U-371* broke through the Straits of Gibraltar in September 1941 soon to be followed by others.

B.d.U. [1] was doubtful whether U-boats would achieve any noteworthy results against the amount and type of shipping found in the Mediterranean and had misgivings about the wisdom of diverting strength from the main "Battle of Merchant tonnage" in the Atlantic. Once in the Mediterranean, U-boats would have to be written off as far as Atlantic employment was concerned.

However the objections were overruled by the High Command who considered the British offensive in North Africa called for the maximum effort by all forces, including U-boats. By the end of 1941 there were 23 boats in the Mediterranean.

(1) Befehlshaber der U.boote (Flag Officer U-Boat), Admiral Karl Donitz.

The opening of hostilities in December 1941 between Germany and the United States caused a further extension of the area of U-boat activities. The returns expected from a campaign in busy waters defended by comparatively weak and inexperienced forces were too good to miss, especially because the growing strength of British convoy escorts had made mid-Atlantic operations less profitable.

B.d.U got only half of the twelve Type IX boats wanted for operations off the American seaboard but when these large boats proved what excellent pickings were to be had, B.d.U shifted all available 500-ton fighting boats westwards to join them.

The decision was strongly influenced by the readiness of the first U-tankers to enable the 500-toners to refuel on their return passage.

The expansion to these three new areas – northern waters, the Mediterranean and the western Atlantic exposed the inadequacy of the results produced by the building programme set in train in the autumn of 1939. It had been appreciated as early as mid-1941 that even if production were to be increased later, time lost at this period could never be recaptured. By December, it was evident that the available U-boats could not prevent decisive supplies reaching Britain, while prospects for improving the building situation were not favourable.

Chart 1 shows the considerable decline in output during the winter of 1941-42 owing to the severe weather in the Baltic coupled to deterioration in the labour and raw materials situation. Charts 3 and 4 show that the size of the fleet continued to grow but this was due more to a gradual decline in the losses percentage rather than an output increase. The growth was not sufficient to provide for the greater operational commitments. Shortage of labour also delayed the final fitting-out and repairing of active-service boats. Basic refits were normally necessary after 15 to 18 months of active service and required a dockyard period of two to three months for the first basic refit and double this time for the second one.

In the autumn of 1941, about 5% of active-service boats were undergoing refits but it was feared that delays might cause the figure to rise to 15% by the end of 1942.

An improvement in the dockyard labour situation had been expected by the autumn of 1941 when decisive victories in the eastern front would release manpower for other employment. However prospects of such victories receded at this time!

By the end of 1942, see Chart 1, the combined efforts of the sixteen yards engaged on U-boat construction with the contribution of a few boats from two others were producing an average of 19 new constructions a month. Not until mid-1943 did the current methods of production, as opposed to pre-fabrication, achieve the monthly average of 20 to 25 boats which Dönitz had declared imperative, and by then the older type of U-boat was already obsolescent.

Only 10% of the programme ordered after the outbreak of war was implemented in 1942. Within the German navy the production of U-boats had been given top priority, but on the whole, the demands of the German army and airforce ranked higher than those of the navy in the overall war production policy. In December 1941 the whole building programme was reviewed on the basis of both the commitments of the various types of U-boats and the demands made upon labour and raw materials. The most that was hoped was an operational fleet of 300 boats by the start of 1944.

However, after their convoy offensive defeat in the spring of 1943, the flow of new boats to the operational fleet was deliberately held back until new weapons and tactics could be perfected. As it turned out the actual figure for the operational fleet by January 1944, was about 170. See Chart 3. The greatest operational fleet increase occurred in 1942, when it more than doubled. By the end of the year there were 164 Atlantic boats in the total of 213. The campaign against the Allied landings in North Africa led to heavy losses and caused the drop after September 1942.

The achievement of a fleet of this size by mid-1942 came nearly 3 years after Dönitz had made such an estimate for really decisive operations, although by then the commitments had greatly extended. There can be no doubt that by the time Germany possessed an adequate U-boat fleet, the most favourable moment for its employment had passed. By the autumn of 1942 the size of the U-boat fleet enabled an all-out offensive against the North Atlantic convoys. This battle, which lasted until May 1943, ended in a decisive defeat for the U-boats. Admiral Dönitz was obliged to withdraw his forces from the North Atlantic and for about four months this area was left practically undisturbed.

May 1943 marked the turning point in the Atlantic battle in the sense that until then the initiative had been held by the Germans, but now passed firmly into Allied hands. The U-boat command spent the succeeding months analysing the reasons for defeat and perfecting new weapons and tactics for the next offensive. It was clear that the dominating factors were, on the one hand the growing strength of the Allied anti-submarine forces, particularly aircraft, and on the other, the Allied radar superiority.

Mention should be made of the Beobachter-dienst, the German naval Intelligence Service, commonly known as the B-dienst, which had such success in deciphering British naval signals, especially diversion signals to convoys at sea. The B-dienst, established before 1939, had already broken Admiralty codes before the war. By the summer of 1940 the B-dienst was reading up to 2000 messages a month but when the Admiralty changed all its ciphers in August 1940, the German crypto-analysts did not break through again until well into 1942. German listening stations existed all over Europe from Finland to a clandestine one in Seville, operated with the connivance of the Spanish government.

The British Merchant Fleet

We now turn to the other topic in this booklet, namely the convoys. We will start with some general information – see Table 2. The pre-war British merchant shipping fleet was the largest in the world. In 1939 it contained nearly one third of the world's merchant ships and almost exceeded the combined total tonnage of its next three rivals – the United States, Japan and Norway – although it should be pointed out that the British fleet had gradually declined in size for some years due to the trade depression of the 1930's while those of her rivals were growing rapidly. Although pay, in pre-war years was abysmally low in proportion to the skills and qualifications required, there was never a shortage of young men anxious to be apprentices or cadets. The apprentice Indentures were strict and one company even laid down that the boy "should not frequent ale houses or taverns"! It can be mentioned that visits to certain other types of establishment were apparently not viewed with the same disapproval!

When Germany occupied half of Europe after the "blitzkriegs" of 1940 and 1941, a large proportion of the merchant ships from the occupied countries were at sea and escaped capture. The BBC immediately put out broadcasts offering protection to these ships and payment for their services. At the same time, rival appeals purporting to come from the ship-owners, but in reality broadcast by the Germans, urged Masters to return to their home ports. Partly because these broadcasts began with the words "My dear Master" – a form of address the ship-owners would not have used and partly due to the appeals of a well-respected Norwegian ship owner, Mr Hhysing Olsen, the Masters sailed to Allied controlled ports. The same procedure was adopted when Holland and Belgium were attacked a month later. Not one ship from these countries went back to the Germans. In 1941 a fresh supply of shipping dropped into Britain's lap when Greece and Yugoslavia were invaded. The large Greek fleet made a most valuable contribution.

It may seem surprising that neutral ships were risked when their owners sent them to work for the British. The main country affected was Sweden which offered 60% of her cargo fleet outside the Baltic. Thus Britain received another 480 thousand tons of much-needed shipping. Britain's astute actions brought over 700 merchant ships from occupied countries. These, with the neutral Swedes, provided an extra 3 million tons of priceless shipping capacity, a 25% increase in her effective fleet.

The Convoys in March 1943

Two particular convoys, HX.229 and SC.122, are now considered. These sailed in March 1943 from Halifax, Nova Scotia to Liverpool. This booklet is restricted to a single pair of convoys for two main reasons and several more minor inclinations. In the first place, there is a superb source document detailing the story from both sides. Not the least impressive feature of this book is the very detailed research undertaken in its compilation. Written by Martin Middlebrook, it is entitled "Convoy". It is a book that the reader is loath to put aside such is the compelling narrative. I commend it to be read in the full. The second reason is that these convoys occurred at a significant turning point in a battle.

However before embarking on this awesome tale, a significant point on the immediately preceding convoy should be mentioned. Convoy HX.228 was the first trans-Atlantic convoy to have an American carrier in the escort. In the summer of 1943 the U.S.S. "Bogue" achieved fame in hunting down U-boats in the middle Atlantic, but over HX.228, whether because of inexperience or poor weather, its aircraft seem to have made little impression on the U-boats. No U-boat reported an attack by carrier aircraft during the operation.

When very long-range land-based aircraft began to appear over our convoys on 11 March 1943, the effect on the shadowing U-boats was immediate and decisive. Their contact was lost on the morning of the 11th, briefly regained twice during the day, but lost for good about 1600 hrs. only twenty-six hours after first sighting the convoy. For the next two days U-boats searched in vain. This successful defence was an instance of the steadily growing effectiveness of air cover for American-United Kingdom convoys.

The U-boat Groups

The attack on HX.229 and SC.122 represents the high point of convoy operations not only in March 1943, but in the entire battle of the Atlantic. German preparations were as near perfect as possible. The "B" service supplied intelligence both on originally planned routes and diversions ordered during passage.

Three U-boat groups were involved in the encounter:-

RAUBGRAF - which translates as "Robber Baron"
STÜRMER - "Daredevil"
DRÄNGER - "Harrier" in the sense of harassing.

The latter consisted of eleven boats of the former "Neuland" group called back from pursuit of H.228. The first named group waited off Newfoundland with the other two in mid-Atlantic where they hoped for a larger scale repetition of the effective encircling manoeuvre used against SC.121. About forty U-boats assaulted the two convoys, the largest number yet to participate in an operation. As so often happened, despite current intelligence and careful dispositions, the first contact was purely chance, by a U-boat en route to a re-fuelling rendezvous. However, the approximately accurate placing of the U-boat groups on the basis of intelligence permitted the chance contact to be quickly exploited.

The inherent confusion in convoy warfare was shown by B.d.U's difficulty, in spite of his advance information, in determining from the U-boat reports which convoy was being attacked. The two convoys were fairly close together in mid-ocean and were treated by the German command as separate parts of a single target. Finally, the weakening of escorts due to the increased number of ships convoyed in March is striking in the case of HX.229 and SC.122. Both convoys were very large, and both were guarded by too few escorts to cope with the assault by the "Wolf-packs". Damaged ships had to be abandoned, presenting U-boats with helpless targets. Air cover during daylight hours on the 17th and the 19th, forced temporary loss of contact, but could not dampen the fighting mood of the U-boats or drive them out of striking range. Certainly the U-boats had tenacity, even if B.d.U. exaggerated the commendation in his decrypted message of 21st April.

"Thanks and appreciation for the greatest convoy success so far. After the wonderful surprise blow achieved on the first night, resolute and energetic pursuit in spite of strong air and sea defence has brought you fine successes in day and night attacks".

The success against H.229 and SC.122 stands out as the last display of aggressive power and spirit by the U-boats. From then until the withdrawal of the "Wolf-packs" from the north Atlantic at the end of May, there was a decline in the ability of U-boats to seize opportunities and drive home the attack. This change is seen in the failure of the subsequent operation against HX.230 where most of the prerequisites for success were present. The route of the convoy was accurately anticipated and the groups, "SEEWOLF" and "SEETEUFEL", totalled about forty boats south-east of Cape Farewell. Despite confusion due to an unsuccessful attempt by the "SEETEUFEL" group to operate on a westbound convoy, the U-boats were in a position to close HX.230 when contact was made on 27th March about 100miles south east of Cape Farewell. This allowed ample space for a running fight lasting several days. Yet by noon of the 28th not a single U-boat operating had maintained contact during the entire operation and only three boats got close enough to fire. The convoy lost one straggler.

A main reason for the U-boat failures was the strengthening of the escort by a support group that joined after contact was made. This was a new British policy, compelled by the heavy losses earlier in the month, of groups of Home Fleet destroyers formed into mobile additional escort units which could go from convoy to convoy, accompanying each one through the greatest danger zone. The numerous reports from U-boats driven off by depth-charge attacks on 28th March are evidence of the efficiency of the strengthened escort.

A Benefit from the Wolf-pack Tactic

The fearsomely named "Wolf-pack" tactic did have one essential element that the Allies turned to their benefit. For a successful pack attack, the U-boats had to use wireless to report the sighting of a convoy and to send off shadowing reports to enable other boats to join. The Germans even used wireless to report attack results, their stock of fuel and torpedoes and for weather reports. They realised the Allies would pick up these signals and take cross-bearings from two stations to roughly locate the U-boat, but they believed such "fixes" were not accurate and accepted a slight risk of being located. In fact in 1942, the Allies fitted a ship-borne high frequency direction finder (HF/DF or "Huff-duff" for short) to a proportion of escorts. As a result a U-boat signalling near a convoy could be "fixed" with great accuracy and thus hunted. This relatively simple device caused the destruction of numerous U-boats in the following years. Kapitan Hans Meckel, staff officer in charge of U-boat signals, has recorded that one of the German naval intelligence branches knew all about Huff-duff early in its existence and had passed a danger warning to U-boat headquarters. This was contained in a routine report but its importance was not appreciated by the officer reading the report. As the intelligence branch never followed up its warning, action was never taken on it!

A former U-boat commander has related how he and other Captains only responded to the third request for weather reports because they knew that three days' silence meant their relatives being informed that their boats were presumed sunk.

Convoys HX.229 and SC.122

Let us now move to those perilous early months of 1943. It would be difficult to improve upon Captain Roskill's words to describe the situation of early 1943 in Volume II of "The War at Sea".

"Thus was the stage set for Germany to fling into the Atlantic struggle the greatest possible strength, directed by the man who had from the beginning of the war controlled the U-Boats and had always been their protagonist. It was plain to both sides that the U-boats and the convoy escorts would shortly be locked in a deadly, ruthless series of fights in which no mercy would be expected and little shown…..In all the long history of sea warfare there has been no parallel to this battle".

On Monday 1 March there were over one hundred fully loaded merchant ships in New York's upper bay and the Hudson river to form convoys to England. The successful "Operation Torch" in North Africa the previous November meant the Germans' days there were numbered. There were preparations for the invasion of Sicily in five months time and in England the huge build up for "Overlord" continued. At sea the Royal Navy had survived the desperate battles on the Malta and Russian routes.

In the Pacific the great American counter offensive against the Japanese was gathering momentum. In Russia, the defeat of the Germans at Stalingrad had occurred a month earlier. RAF Bomber Command was about to start the battle of the Ruhr. Finally, the first attempt by the Germans to remove Hitler, with a time-bomb in his aircraft on 13 March was unsuccessful when it failed to explode.

The Allied countries were heartened by progress in every theatre of war except one. The north Atlantic was the only place where the Allies were on the defensive and the outcome still in doubt. In January 1943 not one convoy was discovered by U-boats, this was partly due to winter storms and partly because the route planners sent convoys on longer evasive routes and finally changed Admiralty codes. Thus the B-dienst could not read the signals diverting convoys away from U-boat concentrations. In January, only one north Atlantic convoy was attacked and it lost only one ship. February was different, two misfortunes occurred to augment the breaking of the new codes by the B-dienst and five convoys were caught and attacked. Britain used 750,000 tons more imports than arrived in the battered convoys. The battle of the Atlantic was near.

The convoys that gathered in New York were basically of two types – 'slow' and 'fast'. The dividing mark was a speed of 10 knots but the average speed for a slow convoy was about 7 knots while a 'fast' one would make 9 knots. The former were usually sailing at roughly eight or nine-day intervals and 'fast' ones on a weekly basis. The code designations given to convoys were "HX" for fast eastbound from Halifax, Nova Scotia, "SC" for slow eastbound from Sydney, Cape Breton Island, "ON" and "ONS" were Outward North Atlantic and Outward North Atlantic Slow.

The Chart 6 shows the original routes for SC.122, HX.229 and HX.229a. The compromise was between minimum lack of air cover, freedom to divert northward to avoid U-boats but avoiding the iceberg area and minimum distance on the great circle route. Before 1943, convoys had taken only thirty merchant ships but with the build-up at New York and advice coupled to a larger escort, sixty-four ships were formed into SC.122 and the eighty faster ships split equally between HX.229 with the fastest, largest and most valuable ships in HX.229a. Fifteen escort vessels took the three convoys out of New York, five more would join before Newfoundland.

The Convoys set out

With thirty-one ships at Halifax, a total of 141 ships stood ready to sail across the Atlantic in the three convoys. The combined gross weight was approximately 860 thousand tons with 920 thousand tons of cargo – 170 thousand tons of various petroleum fuels, 150 thousand tons of frozen meat and 600 thousand tons of general cargo such as food, raw materials, bombs, shells, lorries, locomotives, aircraft and tanks.

Early on 5 March SC.122 was on the move out of New York. By late afternoon it had reformed into eleven columns which would be augmented to thirteen by the ships joining from Halifax.

The first night passed without incident. Weather the next day was fair and the convoy covered about 160 miles in the first twenty-four hours out of New York. The Greek ship GEORGIOS P, built in 1903 and loaded with sugar was the second oldest ship in the convoy. She was unable to keep up and was ordered back to New York by Captain White R.N.R., the Convoy Commodore.

During the late afternoon of the first full day at sea the weather deteriorated and a full scale gale soon ensued. One of the Canadian officers on their open bridges described such storms as "sheert unmitigated hell". At dawn the following day SC.122 was scattered over many miles of ocean. When the storm abated, escorts started to shepherd the merchant ships back into order, helped by a pre-arranged, noon-time rendezvous. Although eleven of the forty-nine merchant ships were missing, this experience was nothing out of the ordinary and fortunately none of the missing ships had sunk. Two returned to New York and six made their way to Halifax, one for repair to a 15-foot crack in her deep tank. Two others caught up a couple of days later and one of these was the Dutch ship KEDOE, whose rejoining caused some interest on the Commodore's bridge. They could scarce believe their eyes as they watched this little ship battle against the elements to regain her correct station. Before the Commodore left the bridge he told the signaller to send "Well done. Look up Luke 15 : 6". Verse 6 of St Luke's gospel runs**"and when he cometh home, he calleth together his friends and neighbours, saying unto them, 'rejoice with me, for I have found my sheep that was lost".** A couple of hours later there was a frantic reply from the Dutch Master "I cannot find it in my Confidential Books!!" It was never ascertained whether the Master had indeed been searching the Confidential Books or whether he just had a sense of humour!

Three days after SC.122 left New York, the forty ships in HX.229 sailed and a day later the extra convoy HX.229a left with a further twenty-seven ships and with seven, had the largest escort of all three convoys. Both convoys missed the gale that dispersed SC.122 but were troubled by fog. When this lifted only eight ships were found to be still with the Commodore, but most soon caught up and only three fell out for good. On the fourth day the convoys reached the Halifax Ocean Meeting Point abbreviated as "HOMP". On 8 March fourteen ships were ready to sail from Halifax to join SC.122. After various changes fifty-one ships and five escorts sailed on as SC.122 under the command of the young Lieutenant Campbell RN, Captain of HMS Leamington. While the three convoys approached Newfoundland, events elsewhere would affect the fortunes of the convoys.

All through the winter Dönitz persisted with his policy of concentrating his U-boats on the North Atlantic convoy routes. New boats coming into service continued to exceed losses and with at least one supply boat in the air gap, Dönitz was able to keep nearly fifty U-boats organised in three patrol lines on these routes. But this was a peak.

The predecessors of our convoys, SC.121 and HX.228 were both caught by such groups although SC.121, on the northern route managed to pass unseen through a patrol line but was spotted soon afterwards by a lone U-boat. The seventeen-boat "WESTMARK" group pursued the convoy for four days and sank thirteen ships without loss to themselves. Chart 7 shows the situation at midnight 10 – 11 March

1943 and the impending dangers gathering against the convoys. All convoys passed through the area east and north-east of Newfoundland which was something of a bottleneck. Dönitz tried to keep one group in this area even though it was within the radius of Allied aircraft. It was RAUBGRAF with fourteen boats now on station, searching for an incoming convoy, ONS.169. Severe weather helped evade the U-boats but fourteen of the thirty seven ships became stragglers.

The German Assessment

The German codebreakers of the B-dienst were at work and U-boat headquarters already had a message for the sailing date of HX.229a on 9 March, the convoy's future route, the straggler's route and the positions of its Halifax and St John's meeting points. The details were correct except that the Germans believed the convoy was HX.229 and when they found HX.229 had sailed on the 8th they complained it sailed a day early! It was most unusual for the B-dienst to get a complete route in this way which seems to have occurred because a copy of the message, normally sent by land-line, was later transmitted by wireless to the Senior Officer Present Afloat (SOPA), off Greenland. There are 8 accurate reports about SC.122 and HX.229 in the B-dienst papers but none for HX.229a. So perhaps that escort managed without sending signals or perhaps the methodical Germans, expecting only two convoys, only looked for signals about two convoys. So as the convoys approached Newfoundland, the staff officers at U-boat headquarters knew that two convoys were on the move, they had the complete future route of one and an accurate record of the progress of SC.122 and HX.229 between New York and Newfoundland. They did not realise that an extra convoy had sailed and they had no future routes for two of the convoys.

The Convoy Escort

The headquarters of Western Approaches in Liverpool was responsible for the provision of the escort groups. At St Johns each group was supposed to have two clear days for rest and repairs before joining an England-bound convoy. A minor crisis was brewing here that would affect the future fortunes of the three convoys. The Western Approaches programme listed B5 group to take over SC.122 on 12 March, and B4 group to take over HX.229 on 14 March. The extra convoy, HX.229a, was to be escorted by 40th escort group, specially sent from England and was to be ready to take over the duty on 15 March. For this run the B5 group comprised two destroyers, a new frigate and five corvettes. In command of the B4 group was Commander ECL Day in HMS HIGHLANDER, a Havant class destroyer. The group was depleted at this time, one destroyer was refitting and its replacement was under repair in Iceland. He had only four instead of the normal six corvettes.

To add to these troubles, by the time the group was due to sail HIGHLANDER would be in dry dock with serious leaks, one corvette was delayed by engine trouble and two others would still be at sea escorting the remnants of ONS.169. Hurried steps were taken to reinforce B4 group and the escort for HX.229 comprised four destroyers and one corvette ready to sail with one destroyer and three corvettes able to sail and catch up before the main U-boat area was reached. The 40th Group had three 900-ton sloops, two large 1,546-ton ex-US coastguard cutters on loan to the Royal Navy and two 1,045-ton frigates. It was thus a modern fast, large escort group in contrast to the mainly old destroyers and slow corvettes of the B4 and B5 groups.

The three convoys were escorted by seven destroyers, nine corvettes, three frigates, two sloops, two cutters and one trawler, although not all were yet ready to sail. The most experienced group commander would be left behind, hoping to catch up when HIGHLANDER'S repairs were complete. Some of these twenty-four ships would soon face a greater concentration of U-boats than had ever before threatened the North Atlantic convoy routes.

Part of the daily routine in the ship's mess reads like a Dickensian depiction of 19th century social conditions.

The *"no need to dress as we slept in our clothes"* can be understood in such potentially dangerous conditions: but it goes on *"the first one to rise made the tea which was the only good thing about breakfast, the bread, biscuits and jam was a help-yourself arrangement. The bread had to be vigorously shaken, - to rid it of cockroaches"*.

The midday meal usually took the form of what was called 'pot mess' which was tinned stewing steak, peas, beans and fresh potatoes with sufficient water to cover this concoction"

As it happened, three of the escorts were strangers to their groups and were destined to affect the fortunes of their respective convoys, although in widely differing ways. Temporary command of HX.229 rested with HMS VOLUNTEER and SC.122's escort had both the trawler CAMPOBELLO and the destroyer UPSHUR. The ASDIC cones and the 4000 yard radar range of the escort defence arrangements are shown on Chart 8. The Germans had tracked the CAMPOBELLO to St Johns through signals decoded by the B-dienst.

Planning the U-boat Dispositions

While the convoys steamed on there was much activity at the intelligence centres and operations rooms in Berlin, London, Washington and Halifax. Signals were intercepted and deciphered, new plans made and changed, countermove followed move. Both sides had only partial knowledge of the other's intentions. The war diary of U-boat headquarters had the following entry for 12 March 1943:

"on the basis of decoded messages received from B-dienst, the leadership decided to commence the operation against HX.229 which had been detected".

This initiated the formation of STÜRMER and DRÄNGER by the evening of 14th – two days hence. RAUBGRAF maintained position in the convoy-route bottleneck. Dönitz harnessed the entire force of U-boats in the North Atlantic for one massive operation against HX.229, displayed on Chart 9 and based on the excellent intelligence about that convoy from a deciphered route diversion message from Halifax at 16:16 on 12th. Dönitz had the text within two hours and knew the position, course and speed. He intended RAUBGRAF to catch HX.229 and the other two patrol lines could dash across and join the affray. If HX.229 diverted eastwards then the 600-mile line of STÜRMER and DRÄNGER would still form a barrier right down the centre of the north Atlantic. The only fault in Dönitz's intelligence was that it related to HX.229a not HX.229 but this was close enough to HX.229's route. On the 12th, the same day Dönitz was preparing to trap HX.229, Washington altered plans for SC.122 at the regular morning meeting to assess convoy and estimated U-boat positions.

Fate now took a cruel twist. On this morning the estimate based on DF's was:-
"20 U-boats patrolling between 50N, 38W and 56N, 46W".

This is RAUBGRAF and is plotted on Chart 9, **but it stretched across some 1,200-miles**, right across the position that SC.122 would reach in two days. RAUBGRAF was actually only 600-miles, but also, as can be seen, SC.122 would possibly have just missed it! Four U-boats that had recently left for home base and signalled from well to the south-west of the line probably caused the error.

The decision to re-route SC.122 caused the following signal:-
"amend route from position 48.22, 46.50 to 57.10, 46.50"

The next day this sent SC.122 on a long diversion northwards but further developments altered the plan yet again.

At this juncture a RAUBGRAF boat reported sighting the westbound ON.170 to U-boat Headquarters. The group closed in on this convoy and sank one merchant ship, in bad weather and then lost contact. However this meant that the Americans now knew the exact location of the RAUBGRAF boats. Signals were quickly sent to divert SC.122 and HX.229 well to the east. HX.229a was still some distance from the danger but a diversion was ordered further north around the other side of the danger area. B-dienst deciphered these signals and U-boat headquarters had the texts within four hours. These and earlier texts gave Dönitz's staff an accurate idea of where the two leading convoys were at the time and also their future movements. However it was twelve hours later, on the afternoon of 14th before the RAUBGRAF group had orders to move south east at top speed towards SC.122. The intention to concentrate against the one convoy HX.229, was now extended to an attempt to catch both SC.122 **and** HX.229. This is shown on Chart 10.

The delay meant that U-boat headquarters had miscalculated the convoy's progress and RAUBGRAF lost all chance of getting ahead of SC.122 although it would menace HX.229.

U-boats that had been on patrol for some time needed to refuel and would normally operate well beyond their own fuel capacity. This was a great act of faith in the U-boat headquarters staff officers who controlled the tanker U-boats. At this time there were two of these in the air gap. Operational U-boats added a small coded message in signals to headquarters to indicate their fuel stocks in cubic metres and the boat was ordered to a rendezvous when fuel ran low. This facility undoubtedly enabled a large number of U-boats to be kept at sea.

A total of 42 U-boats would become involved in the coming convoy operation although not all would succeed in making contact. Ten of the 37 standard Type Vllc boats were on their first patrol as were five of the larger Type lXc boats, en-route to Biscay bases. The patrol line was a well tried feature of U-boat operations by this time. The system depended on centralised control by Headquarters and U-boat seamanship skills. Dönitz's staff would send a signal to boats giving the Gruppe code-name and each boat's position in the line-up, the position of the ends, the time of assembly, the speed and direction of sweep. Later signals to the Gruppe might amend the direction and speed of the sweep. Each individual boat would plot its own part in it. The distance between boats was about 20 sea miles. Signals came from Nauen which was exclusively reserved for U-boat signals. There was also a station at Kalbe with a powerful very-low frequency transmitter that could reach U-boats submerged to 15 metres. The boats were not in touch with each other. There was no Gruppe control boat and once a patrol line was established radio silence was kept unless a convoy was seen.

The Initial Bouts

March 15th was a day when the convoys were more affected by a bad storm than by the Germans. The slower convoy, SC.122 still led HX.229 but now by only just over half a day's steaming. See Chart 10. The storm separated the 545-ton HMS CAMPOBELLO and the 775-ton Icelandic ship SELFOSS from SC.122. The Captain and First Mate on SELFOSS decided to make straight for their Icelandic destination and in fact sailed right through one of the biggest U-boat concentrations of the war without being spotted. After six days and sailing alone for almost 1,000 miles they arrived safely in Reykjavik. HMS CAMPOBELLO was not so lucky. She struggled to maintain her place with a very bad leak somewhere under the coal bunkers. It was eventually abandoned and deliberately sunk. Thus the escort lost a brand new ship coupled to a delay until HMS GODETIA sent back to help, could rejoin the convoy and the signal she sent gave the B-dienst another accurate fix on SC.122's position, course and speed at the time.

The storm had actually pushed the ships of HX.229 over 10 knots in a direction that was almost a direct route to England. Commander Luther ordered a signal to "Convoy & Routeing" requesting a route on a direct line rather than the turn north-east he was due to take in a few hours. There is no record that B-dienst either picked up or made use of this signal but the Admiralty, realised that both HX.229 and SC.122 were only a few hours from the 35 degrees West longitude line where they took over control and they urged such a direct route even though they had a good idea of the presence of the STÜRMER and DRÄNGER patrol lines. Such routeing implied the Admiralty were prepared to give up further attempts to send HX.229 and SC.122 around the huge patrol line and was recommending the two convoys should attempt to fight their way through it to the nearest air cover and on the shortest route to England. "Convoy & Routeing" received this bold suggestion at 18:00 hrs. on 15th but did not order any further changes for another 19 hours by which time the situation altered yet again.

At midnight on 15th the slow convoy, SC.122 was steering east-north-east, well ahead of RAUBGRAF but still facing the formidable 600-mile line of the two other groups, sweeping towards them but still 300 miles to the east. The faster HX.229 managed to evade the RAUBGRAF group, for the second time, and steamed on an easterly course. Both convoys were forced deeper into the air gap and trapped between two hungry packs of U-boats. The more valuable ships of HX.229a, together with three westbound convoys travelled the northern route in apparent safety.

The Middle Rounds

A RAUBGRAF boat, U.653, was low on fuel, with only a single but defective torpedo. Five crew members had been washed out of the conning tower in a storm the previous month and a petty officer was ill. In this sorry state, U.653 made its way on the surface to rendezvous with a tanker en route to Brest. On the bridge, a light was seen and it was suddenly realised this was a sailor lighting a cigarette on the deck of an adjacent steamer! By the time the Captain arrived on the bridge, the U-boat could see about twenty ships all around them. They did an emergency dive and could hear the engine noises as the convoy passed over them. They surfaced after two hours to send a sighting signal and then took up a shadowing position. U.653 had sailed right into the middle of HX.229, got off its short sighting report of three morse letters and in the morning of 16th, calmly shadowed the convoy – all without being spotted!

U-boat headquarters received the report at 08:25 which gave an accurate convoy position and the great benefit of a shadow in place. Doubtless everyone at U-boat headquarters was delighted to receive U.653's sighting report at the right time and place – dawn in the air gap – to allow other U-boats to join before dark and make a pack attack that night. It was believed that U.653 had sighted SC.122 and that HX.299 was following whereas the real SC.122 was 150 miles ahead and somewhat to the north. Dönitz expected to have four days and nights which was ample time to find the second convoy and strike a double blow. See Chart 11.
He ordered all eight boats in the RAUBGRAF patrol to make top speed towards the convoy from only 80 miles away. Two more joined from a refuelling tanker. Although still 420 miles ahead, he ordered eleven boats from the centre of the STÜRMER-DRÄNGER line to make for the convoy and the remaining STÜRMER boats to turn

south as a back-up. Within about an hour of U.653's sighting report, twenty-one U-boats were making for HX.229. A further message arrived at U-boat headquarters and caused some consternation. This was the two-day old signal to HX.229a ordering the convoy to divert west of the old RAUBGRAF area. B-dienst failed to appreciate that the signal referred to HX.229a and the copy passed to Dönitz on the afternoon of 16 March reported that HX.229 was now north-east of Newfoundland on a northerly course, in complete contrast to previous decodes! This confused the U-boat staff officers who now assumed there was only one convoy in the U.653 area. There was thus no need to keep the remaining STÜRMER-DRÄNGER line to search for the other convoy. All were now ordered to make for the convoy being shadowed. See Chart 12. It is probable that at no other time in the war had such numbers of U-boats been directed onto one convoy. During the rest of the day, 16 March, more U-boats joined to shadow HX.229 and some sighting reports were deciphered and passed to the Admiralty who advised the convoy that it was being shadowed. By 19:00 hours, seven U-boats were now in contact. Chart 13 shows the situation on the morning of 17 March.

About 130 miles north-east, the slower SC.122 had a much quieter day. Two American escorts set out from Iceland, some 900 miles away. When the eleven STÜRMER U-boats had been ordered to make for HX.229, their course would pass close to SC.122 and although the HF/DF picked up U-boat signals during the afternoon, no U-boat appears to have made contact with convoy. So it had a lucky escape but it must have been close.

In HX.229, the stream of U-boat signals coming out of the darkness on the horizon left the Commander in no doubt about the presence of a strong U-boat pack. One patrolling aircraft that evening could have put down every one of the U-boats but alas this was the air gap and not a single v.l.r. aircraft had been allocated to this part of the north Atlantic. By the close of day, thirty-seven merchant ships and four escorts in HX.229 were on a direct 055 degrees course for England with seven U-boats in contact.

Dönitz's staff, who believed HX.229 was the convoy SC.122 ordered the U-boat attack. U.603 had been on patrol for seven weeks, three of the four torpedoes left were the new sophisticated FAT type [Feder-Apparat-Torpedo] which could run right through a convoy, then turn 180 degrees and run back, possibly making several runs until hitting a ship.

While the U-boat Captain watched from up top, the First Watch officer was at his post in the interior of the conning tower at the UZO, the special sighting glass used for U-boat surface attack, connected to the torpedo calculator and built into the front of the conning tower. The oft-filmed U-boat Captain, dramatically positioned at his periscope, was not a feature of the surfaced night attack. The U.603's radio operator sent the obligatory warning signal to other U-boats in the vicinity that FAT torpedoes were to be fired. These boats kept out of the way for at least twenty minutes. The four torpedoes, in two salvos, were fired at 20:00 hours. Only one torpedo found its target, possibly because the convoy had just completed its last turn before dark. The Norwegian ELIN K had only forty men on board and sank very quickly but all the crew got away in lifeboats.

The fourth and last ship in ELIN'S line was a Dutch cargo ship, TERKOELEI, but despite the order for the last ship in any column to act as rescue ship, she sailed straight past the lifeboats without stopping. The stoic Norwegians settled down for a long voyage in their two lifeboats as they perceived that they might not be rescued. Fortunately one of the escorts sighted the two lifeboats as she completed the standard radar and ASDIC sweep of their sector. No U-boat was detected.

Nothing else happened in the next hour but hopes that the U-boat that sank the ELIN had been a "loner" were dashed by a four torpedo attack, two of them FATs at 21:25 hours by U.758., which had been in contact for over twelve hours. The U-boat did not need to penetrate the escort screen because the only escort on the starboard side was the one now picking up the Norwegians from ELIN. So the difficulties encountered at St John's in making up the escort group for this convoy, the absence of a rescue ship and the failure of the Dutch ship to stop and pick up the crew of the ELIN K had now all snowballed to result in the sinking of a Dutch cargo ship ZAANLAND and an American liberty ship JAMES OGLETHORPE. The liberty ship remained afloat, possibly because her cotton cargo swelled and prevented too much water from entering but the damaged steering sent her round in huge circles, narrowly missing the six lifeboats, as the convoy slowly disappeared. As well as this drama, the escort corvette ANEMONE spotted a surfaced U-boat some 3,000 yards away. For twelve minutes the corvette pounded down on the U-boat which failed to see the approaching danger until ANEMONE was only 300 yards away. Although the subsequent heavy depth charge attack failed to destroy U.89, the U-boat gave up hope of attacking the convoy and set course for a tanker. In addition, another U-boat, U.664, had been near enough to be shaken by the depth charges and pulled out of the operation.

Leiutenant-Commander Luther in VOLUNTEER was the only escort to remain with convoy and he decided to sweep the rear of the convoy. To his dismay he found the merchant ship WILLIAM EUSTIS listing heavily to starboard as the crew took to the lifeboats. The U-boat responsible was U.435.

Luther was left with the difficult choice of hunting for the U-boat himself, staying to protect the convoy from further attack or stopping to pick up survivors. After a check sweep he slowed to pick up the seamen. He was not pleased to hear that code books had not been dumped and fired four depth charges as he passed at speed. Survivors told him the cargo was 7,000 tons of sugar so he had just sunk three weeks sugar ration for the whole of Great Britain.

Three U-boats made attacks on HX.229 in three hours and four merchant ships had been torpedoed. The situation at 23:00 could be seen as a moment of crisis for the convoy. Three escorts were absent rescuing survivors, the convoy was completely without escort and would remain so for a further hour and a half. Finally although six

U-boats were in contact in perfect weather conditions for surface attack, not one torpedo was fired at the convoy in that time. Midnight came and perhaps the seamen of Irish extraction wondered what St Patrick's day would bring. Within a short while two further escorts rejoined the convoy but so did two further U-boats. Three-quarters of an hour past midnight ended the immunity when two torpedoes hit the HARRY LUCKENBACH even though she had been pursuing her own zig-zag course. The freighter went down in four minutes. Ten torpedoes were fired at the convoy. The Captain of U.435 was perhaps over enthusiastic in his success signal which detailed five ships he had hit although his torpedoes had actually hit nothing at all! Although the HARRY LUCKENBACK went down quickly, enough of her crew managed to get away to fill three lifeboats which were seen three miles behind the convoy. The escort captain involved felt he could not leave the convoy with only the radar-less MANSFIELD as escort and reported the lifeboats to the Convoy Commander so that one of the other escorts coming up from astern could deal with the survivors. Four possible rescue ships all passed by these lifeboats. As a result of this agonising series of events not one man of the HARRY LUCKENBACH was ever seen again and it will never be known how they all perished.

St Patrick's Day

There was now an hour and a half lull until danger came at 02:18 when U.616 which had tried to get a shot at the convoy for over an hour saw the escort ship BEVERLY heading straight ftowards her. Four torpedoes were fired at the destroyer but her high speed and erratic zig-zag saved her and no one aboard was ever aware of the great danger. An hour and a half before first light U.600 fired a much-delayed salvo of five torpedoes from ahead of the starboard columns and hit three ships – IRENEE DU PONT, an American freighter, the British refrigerated ship NARIVA and the 12,000 tons tanker SOUTHERN PRINCESS which was the largest ship in the convoy with a cargo of 10,000 tons of fuel oil and a couple of railway engines. The oil soon caught fire and it was a miracle that only four of the 100 men on board did not get away safely, many were rescued by the New Zealand ship TEKOA. The rescue ships were in fact in great danger because no less than five U-boats were attracted to the blazing tanker but the six torpedoes fired at the group either missed or hit an already stricken ship. So by God-given fortune the three rescue ships survived and for four nervous hours plucked 240 oil-covered survivors from the sea, by which time it was daylight.

The convoy Commodore adopted a sequence of "emergency turns" which he recorded as "having the desired effect of disorganising the U-boat plan" – this is a good example of the widespread belief that the Germans were acting under one U-boat captain, whereas actually they were taking part in a confused free-for-all. During this time the BEVERLY got a good Radar and ASDIC contact with a U-boat, the depth charge attack severely shook U.228 and caused a small leak. The BEVERLY did not regain contact and left to rejoin the dangerously weak convoy escort. The Commander was later criticised for not remaining longer over the U-boat but this was an easier decision to make afterwards in a Londonderry office than on BEVERLY's bridge. Although there were eight U-boats still in contact with the convoy, seven of these were well astern either repairing or reloading torpedo tubes. Six of the 11 U-boats in the area had fired 28 torpedoes in 8 attacks and hit eight merchant ships. Of the 590 men on the torpedoed ships, 447 were safely rescued.

An interesting coincidence links U.338 to Bletchley Park. When this boat was being prepared for launch at Nordsee Werke at Emden in April 1942, too many of the restraining ropes were cut and the U-boat prematurely launched itself, its first "success" was to sink a small river craft that got in the way. Because of this incident U.338's crew decided to call their boat "the Wild Donkey" and an appropriate symbol was painted on the conning tower. Those who have read the PETARD display panels in Hut 8 at Bletchley Park may recall a U-boat, U.559 with a donkey painted on the conning tower and whose capture played an important part in getting back into the SHARK four-wheel Enigma cipher. U.338 was one of the STURMER boats previously ordered to reach HX.229 on the 17th but while on its way lookouts unexpectedly saw a convoy a mile dead ahead. This was SC.122 on a roughly parallel course 120 miles north-east of HX.229. The escort ship GODETIA was absent after picking up the CAPOBELLO'S crew but seven of the eight escorts were in a standard screen with one ahead of each outer column of the convoy with nothing in between, U.338 had fortuitously passed unseen between the two. Five torpedoes were fired which finished off 4 merchant ships of over 24,000 tons with nearly 30,000 tons of valuable war cargo. 40 British and Dutch seamen were lost in those bleak wastes. Chart 13 shows the situation on the morning of 17 March.

Another STÜRMER boat, U.641, also making for HX.229 mistook a merchant ship's red masthead light for an aircraft and the torpedo explosions as being depth charges and continued its journey towards HX.229 completely unaware that it had been so close to another convoy. A third STÜRMER boat, U.598, had been a few miles to the south and saw the "snowflake" illumination flares fired when U.338 was seen on the convoy and also continued her journey to the south west in search of HX.229.

Thus at the end of this first night of the battle, twelve Allied merchant ships had been lost for just two U-boats slightly damaged. Dawn broke on a somewhat decimated convoy and a scattered and rather embittered escort who felt they had been beaten by facts outside their control and by sheer weight of numbers.

Both Commander Boyle, escort to SC.122 and Lieutenant-Commander Luther, escort to HX.229 sent signals with details of the attacks and plots were brought up to date on both sides of the Atlantic. One of the civilian ladies working at the Admiralty's operational intelligence centre under the Citadel in London was Mrs Gwen Boyle, Commander Boyle's wife. The reader is left to ponder her thoughts at this time.

Although 5 additional vessels were on their way to reinforce both convoy escorts these could not join for at least 24 hours. However requests were made to Aldergrove in

Northern Ireland and Reykjavik in Iceland for v.l.r. Liberators to fly to each convoy as soon as within range. So help seemed in hand rather than at hand.

A stream of signals arrived at Hotel am Steinplatz in Berlin. The total claims for the night had risen to fourteen merchant ships totalling 90,000 tons and a further 6 ships damaged. The true count was that only 12 ships had actually been hit. Dönitz and his staff officers had serious work to do. Had U.338 found another convoy or was navigation at fault? The latter was ruled out and it was assumed that a faster section of what was believed to be SC.122 had been located. So confusion lasted until they received further signals for the speeds of the two parts and then it was realised that SC.122 was 120 miles ahead and on a roughly similar course. See Chart 14. Orders went out in the early afternoon for the northern STÜRMER boats to seach for SC.122 while the southernmost STÜRMER and the DRÄNGER group were to make for the "main" convoy. Later, fresh orders went out to all STÜRMER and DRÄNGER boats to operate against SC.122. By late afternoon roughly equal numbers of U-boats were disposed so as to threaten both convoys for the second phase of the convoy battle. B.d.U. considered that enough boats were allocated to HX.229 and SC.122 and he began the formation of another group – SEETEUFEL, which means "Sea Devil" to engage another convoy, ONSI, off Iceland. The point of this is that the position it would take up would be very close to the route to be taken by HX.229a.

A New Factor Intervenes

U.439 cruised on the surface twenty miles behind and had just come across the burning FORT CEDAR LAKE when an alert lookout spotted a large aircraft approaching from the east. Until this point they had thought themselves quite safe from aircraft so far out in the Atlantic. The lookouts fell down the conning tower ladder and a crash dive ensued! The aircraft had taken off from Aldergrove over eight hours earlier intending to join SC.122 but had flown past the convoy in the darkness. Although the attack on the U-boat did not sink it, it was severely shaken and submerged for the rest of the day. The Liberator went on to find SC.122 and spotted another U-boat – U.338, which we met previously. U.666 also saw the aircraft and dived for half an hour. The Liberator continued to patrol to its fuel limit until 09:15 hrs. Although it had no depth charges left it was still an effective deterrent to the U-boats. The aircraft eventually landed near Londonderry seven hours later having been airborne for eighteen hours and twenty minutes.

The appearance of this aircraft changed the entire complexion of the battle. It not only frustrated the U-boats but it gave a great uplift to the morale in the convoy There was an unfortunate two-hour gap caused by high winds over Ireland before the arrival of the next aircraft. In this time 3 U-boats made a further attack but only 1 out of 4 torpedoes found its mark, partly because of quick reaction by the ships. It was U.338 that made this attack and ASDIC signals attracted depth charge responses which, if not successful, did keep these U-boats away from the convoy.

While these events had been taking place the next aircraft arrived over SC.122 and the rest of the afternoon was quiet even though the Liberator had to leave in mid-afternoon and no replacement arrived for the vital last few hours of daylight. One small development on the 17th concerned U.664 and its special short-wave wireless receiver called a "Radone". Quite by chance, Oberleutnant Adolf Graef picked up the conversations of the escort ships. Realising how useful this could be it was arranged to carry an English-speaking crew member and direction finding equipment on the next voyage. Graef's experiment came to an end on 9th August 1943 when U.664 was stranded out in the Atlantic almost out of fuel following the sinking of one of the German tanker U-boats.

At dawn, on the 17th, convoy HX.229, still in the air-gap, had only 28 out of the original 40 merchant ships that left New York, although TEKOA was catching up after rescue work, as were three of the five escorts. In the next few hours the German U-boats also rebuilt their strength. Although many of the RAUBGRAF boats dropped out, having shot off all their torpedoes or being low in fuel, the first of the STÜRMER and DRÄNGER boats now arrived on the scene. By 10:30 there were ten U-boats in contact with the convoy. Two merchant ships, the TERKOELEI and the CORACERO were torpedoed and sunk shortly afterwards.

It may not have been apparent but the fortunes of HX.229 were actually taking a turn for the better at this time. A short while later the escort BEVERLY spotted two U-boats ahead of the convoy. The subsequent careful attacks severely damaged U.530 whose upper deck was crushed and the steel cladding of the conning tower was "rolled up like a piece of paper". BEVERLY'S activities caused at least two and possibly three other U-boats to lose contact with the convoy. Later, two v.l.r. Liberators made contact with HX.229 and spotted six U-boats. This led to the celebrated signal "Six hearses in sight bearing 180 degrees twenty-five miles" sent at its departure. The nine U-boats sighted and the six attacks made marked an encouraging development. As a result there were possibly only 3 U-boats in contact with HX.229 and only 1 with SC.122. No less than twelve U-boats reported to their headquarters that they were forced to drop out of the operation for various reasons – no torpedoes, fuel shortage, mechanical trouble or depth-charge damage. However this still left 31 U-boats, mostly STÜRMER and DRÄNGER boats as potential threats. At dusk on 17th, SC.122 passed the half-way mark of the crossing while HX.229 was only 90 miles behind.

The seamen in the ships of SC.122 and HX.229 and the crews of 31 U-boats prepared for a second night of battle. The first event that night occurred to SC.122 just after 20:00 hours. Although a radar contact had been made, it came too late and four torpedoes were already to hit two ships – the 8,800 tons PORT AUKLAND and ZOUAVE, were hit. These ships were in the firth and sixth of the convoy's ten columns, so no part of a convoy was safe. The first ship was hit in the starboard side and the second on the port side several minutes later, so that may have been a FAT torpedo turning round and making a second run.

The ensuing three-hour rescue of survivors and responses to ASDIC signals makes a quite harrowing tale in itself but was a typical incident in the Battle of the Atlantic. The recording that two ships had been lost with 15,000 tons of cargo and mail, twenty seamen had died but 140 had been saved to sail again, cannot possibly convey the drama of the rescue work in the heavy storm that raged at this time. The convoy steamed on without further attack to greet the dawn of 18th March with much relief after having expected a bad night.

In HX.229, heavy attacks were also expected during the night but none came. This was the first time since the attacks began that the full 5 escort vessels were at hand. It may seem difficult to understand how 30 aggressive U-boats could have completely lost two large convoys that had made no major course changes. But there are at least three contributory explanations – unexpected air patrols the previous afternoon which disorganised the Germans, secondly the gale-force weather and finally luck which favoured the convoy ships. Many U-boats must have passed close during the night but did not get a sighting. The U-boats did not have radar. By fortunate contrast the bad weather around the convoys was good at Reykjavik and Aldergrove which enabled highly efficient and successful air cover for the day. There had been 6 U-boat sightings and 4 attacks during the continuous 10-hour cover. The deterrent effect was an important factor. The aircraft sent out to cover HX.229 failed to locate it although U-boats were spotted and attacked. Two ships were torpedoed. One had a death toll of 30 out of the 87 on board, the other lost 27 out of 69. For the third night of the battle, in the hope that it would be seen by U-boats just before night-fall, both convoys arranged to change course after dark so that U-boats would be in the wrong place when the convoys returned to the original route at dawn. By dusk on the 18th, 4 more merchant ships had been sunk in the past 24-hours bringing the total lost so far to 19 – 12 from HX.229 and 7 from SC.122. Five U-boats had been damaged.

It is ironic that the order for HX.229 to turn 080 degrees an hour after dusk would actually steam the convoy straight at the U-boats coming up astern of SC.122 in response to U.642's sighting signal even though it had been chased away by the escorts.

The Final Skirmishes

The final phase of this convoy battle from the night of 18th March until reaching England, had the two convoys on roughly parallel course, with HX.229 to the north and soon to pass SC.122. However they were so close that the Germans could rarely be certain which convoy a particular U-boat was operating upon. The Coastal Command air operations increasingly benefited both convoys. The action began at 03:10 and there followed a furious 90 minutes of depth charging and chasing ASDIC contacts. Although U.441 sent five torpedoes at three merchant ships and her Captain was delighted to hear explosions which he recorded as one sinking, a ship set on fire and two others hit, in fact all his torpedoes missed. The explosions were depth charges and the rest of his claims can only have been a figment of his imagination.

The furious action gradually died down. Four of HX.229's escorts had attacked U-boats. Three "Hedgehog" attacks were made and 71 depth charges were dropped. Three U-boats were damaged and many others took prudent flight and remained submerged. By dawn not a single U-boat was in touch with the convoy.

When the escort ship ANEMONE did rejoin the convoy, she had only two depth charges left. She flashed a signal to a nearby destroyer offering to exchange some of her rescued female survivors in return for some of the destroyer's depth charges. The author makes no comment upon the relative equality of this example of enterprising 20th century naval bartering!

While this was going on, other U-boats were nosing around SC.122 and shortly before 05:00 hrs a torpedo found its mark in the old Greek cargo ship CARRAS. All the crew members were rescued.

It was now three days and nights since U.653 had sighted HX.229 and started this encounter between convoy and U-boats. The morning of 19th March brought far better weather although there was the further loss of the MATHEW LUCKENBACH.

This could be said to be due to the Master deciding to leave the convoy, take advantage of his superior speed and attempting to "romp-home" on his own. He was caught by U.527 when some 40 miles ahead of HX.229 which fortunately saw the distress rockets. There was a benefit from all this however in that there were no fewer than five U-boats queuing up to finish off this ship, which meant five less to pay attention to the main convoy. See Chart 14. The rest of the day saw a succession of air attacks on U-boats and the following night passed without further loss. Dönitz and his staff realised that the prospect of a repeat of the intense air cover meant the operation was as good as over and orders went to U-boats in contact to break off at dawn. The subsequent actions were between the aircraft of Coastal Command and the U-boats moving away to the west searching back along the convoy paths for stragglers and other targets of opportunity.

The first clash of the battle had occurred nearly four days earlier and 600 miles to the west but now on the afternoon of 20th March the awesome and gruelling battle of convoys SC.122 and HX.229 was over. See Chart 15.

A Concluding Comment

The reader may be interested to hear how Commodore Mayall of HX.229 finished his report for the Admiralty Trade Division. He wrote "Apart from U-boat attacks, the voyage was fairly average"! The last days of the convoy were anything but "fairly average" for those 11 ships carrying over 1,100 rescued survivors.

Sources:

Griffiths et al. *GC & CS Naval History*
(unpublished, until lately Top Secret Ultra) in 24 volumes.

Hinsley, H &Thomas et al: *British Intelligence in the Second World War.*
Vols. 2. HMSO 1979-88.

Imperial War Museum Photographic Section Archive.

Middlebrook, M: *Convoy, the Battle for Convoys SC.122 and HX.229*
.
Roskill, Captain SW., *The War at Sea*, HMSO, 1954-61.

TABLE 1   U-boat Statastics

Type VII: (Standard Displacement 517 Tons)

Type IX: (Standard Displacement 740 Tons)

	VIIc	IXc
Diving Depth:	309 ft.	330 ft.
Displacement (surfaced):	719 tons	983 tons
Length:	221.5 ft.	237.2 ft.
Beam:	20.5 ft.	22.3 ft.
Draught:	14.9 ft.	14.4 ft.
Fuel (heavy diesel oil) max:	113.5 tons	208.2 tons
Endurance (nautical miles)		
at 10 knots surfaced:	9,700	16,300
at 2 knots submerged:	180	128
Speed		
maximum surfaced:	17.7 kts.	18.3 kts.
maximum submerged:	7.6 kts.	7.3 kts.
Diesels:	2 6-cylinder 4-stroke MAN diesels max.cap. 1,400 h.p.	2 9-cylinder 4-stroke MAN (supercharged) diesels max.cap. 2,200 h.p. (each)
Electric Motors:	2 double BBC max.cap. 375 h.p.	2 double SSW, max.cap. 500 h.p.(each)
Batteries:	2 x 62 cells	2 x 62 cells
Armament		
Torpedo-tubes:	4 bow, 1 stern	4 bow, 2 stern
Capacity:	14 torps.(max.) or 4 torps.+ 16 TMA or 3 torps.+ 24 TMB or 4 torps.+ 10 TMA + 9 TMB	22 torps.(max.) or 44 TMA (max.) or 66 TMB (max.)
Guns:	2-0.79" flak twins	1-1.46" flak 2-0.79" flak twins
Crew:	Total 44	Total 48
Numbers built:	661	141
Building Yards:	Germaniawerft, Kiel Vulkan, Vegesack Flenderwerke, Luebeck Nordseewerke, Emden Flensburger Schiffsbau Howaldtswerke, Kiel Danziger Werft, Danzig Schichau, Danzig Deutsche Werke, Kiel Blohm & Voss, Hamburg Howaldtswerke, Hamburg Stuelcken, Hamburg Naval Dockyard, Wilhelmshaven Deschimag Seebuck,	Deschimag, Bremen Deutsche Werft, Hamburg

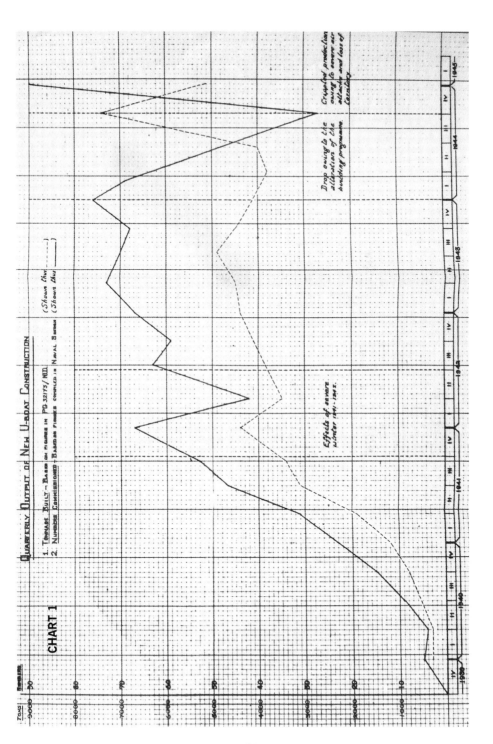

CHART 1

QUARTERLY OUTPUT OF NEW U-BOAT CONSTRUCTION

1. TONNAGE BUILT — BASED ON FIGURES IN PG 32173/NID.   (Shown thus ---------)
2. NUMBER COMMISSIONED — BASED ON FIGURES COMPILED IN NAVAL STAFF.   (Shown thus _____)

Crippled production
owing to severe air
attacks and loss of
territory

Drop owing to the
alteration of the
building programme.

Effects of severe
winter 1941-1942.

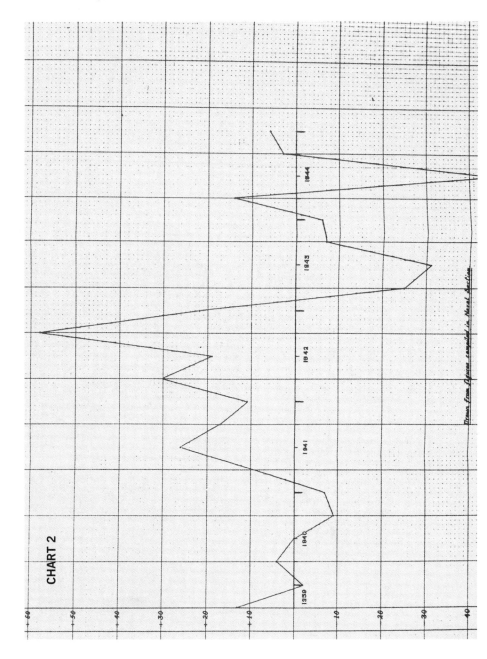

NET QUARTERLY ADDITIONS TO OPERATIONAL U-BOAT FLEET   1939-44

CHART 2

QUARTERLY TOTALS OF U-BOAT FLEET
QUARTERLY TOTALS OF OPERATIONAL U-BOAT FLEET   1939-44

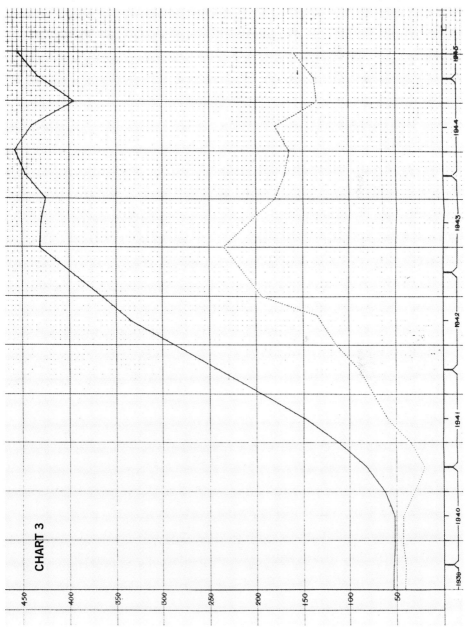

CHART 3

33

A MONTHLY AVERAGES OF BOATS ON OPERATIONS ——— Constructed
B MONTHLY TOTALS OF BOATS LOST ON OPERATIONS ········· the Germans
C "B" AS A PERCENTAGE OF "A" BASED ON A NINE-MONTH MOVING AVERAGE- - - - Naval Section

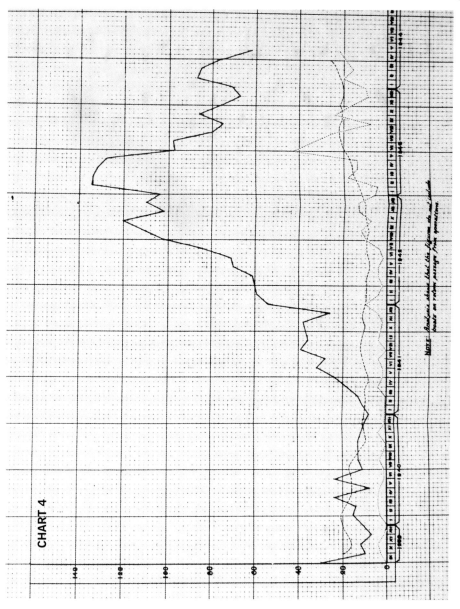

CHART 4

34

CHART 5

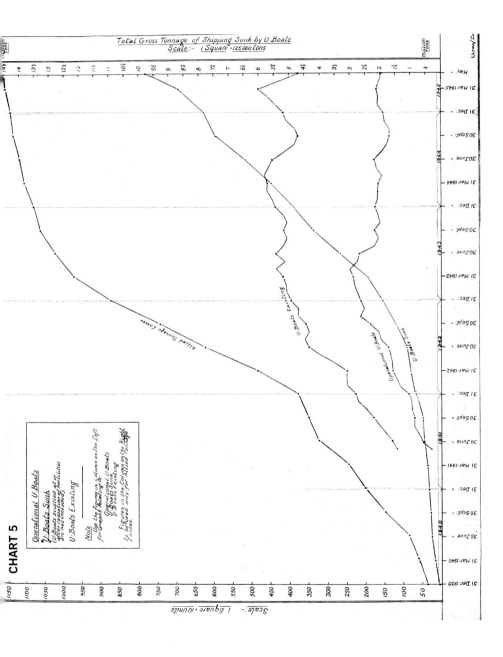

Total Gross Tonnage of Shipping Sunk by U-Boats
Scale:- 1 Square ·125,000 Tons

Operational U-Boats
U-Boats Sunk
(U-Boats scuttled at or after cessation of hostilities are not included)
Operational U-Boats Existing

Note
Use the figures in column on the Left for Graphs Relating to:
Operational U-Boats
U-Boats Sunk
U-Boats Existing
Figures in the Column on the Right to be used only for Allied Tonnage Losses

Allied Tonnage Losses
U-Boats Existing
Operational U-Boats
U-Boats Sunk

Scale:- 1 Square ·10 Units

1150 1100 1050 1000 950 900 850 800 750 700 650 600 550 500 450 400 350 300 250 200 150 100 50

31 Dec.1939 1940 31 Mar.1940 30 June " 30 Sept: " 31 Dec: " 1941 31 Mar.1941 30 June " 30 Sept: " 31 Dec: " 1942 31 Mar.1942 30 June " 30 Sept: " 31 Dec: " 1943 31 Mar.1943 30 June " 30 Sept: " 31 Dec: " 1944 31 Mar.1944 30 June " 30 Sept: " 31 Dec: " 1945 31 Mar.1945 May

14½ 14 13½ 13 12½ 12 11½ 11 10½ 10 9½ 9 8½ 8 7½ 7 6½ 6 5½ 5 4½ 4 3½ 3 2½ 2 1½ 1 ½
Million Tons

TABLE 2

Merchant Fleets Exceeding One Million Gross Tons in 1939

	Nos.of Ships	Gross Tonnage (000) Tonnes
British Empire	2,965	17,524
U.S.A	1,409	8,506
Japan	1,054	5,030
Norway	816	4,209
Germany	713	3,762
Italy	571	3,107
France	502	2,639
Holland	477	2,651
Greece	389	1,663
Russia	299	1,048
Sweden	259	1,040
Total	9,454	51,179

Source- C.B.A. Behrens, Merchant shipping and the Demands of War
H.M.S.O. & Longmans, Green, p23

CHART 6

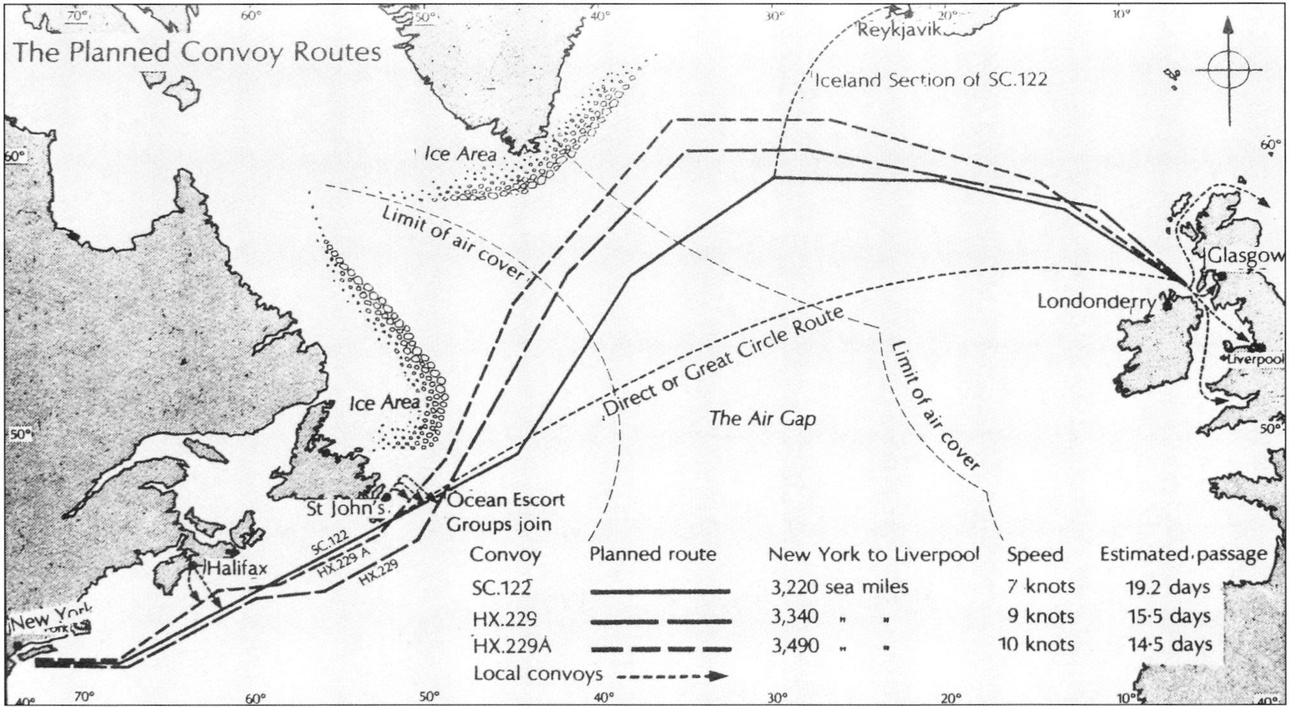

The Planned Convoy Routes

Convoy	Planned route	New York to Liverpool	Speed	Estimated passage
SC.122	(solid line)	3,220 sea miles	7 knots	19.2 days
HX.229	(dashed line)	3,340 " "	9 knots	15.5 days
HX.229A	(long dashed line)	3,490 " "	10 knots	14.5 days
Local convoys	(dash-dot line)			

Glasgow
Liverpool
Londonderry
Reykjavik
Iceland Section of SC.122
Limit of air cover
Direct or Great Circle Route
The Air Gap
Ice Area
Limit of air cover
Ice Area
St John's
Ocean Escort Groups join
Halifax
New York

CHART 7

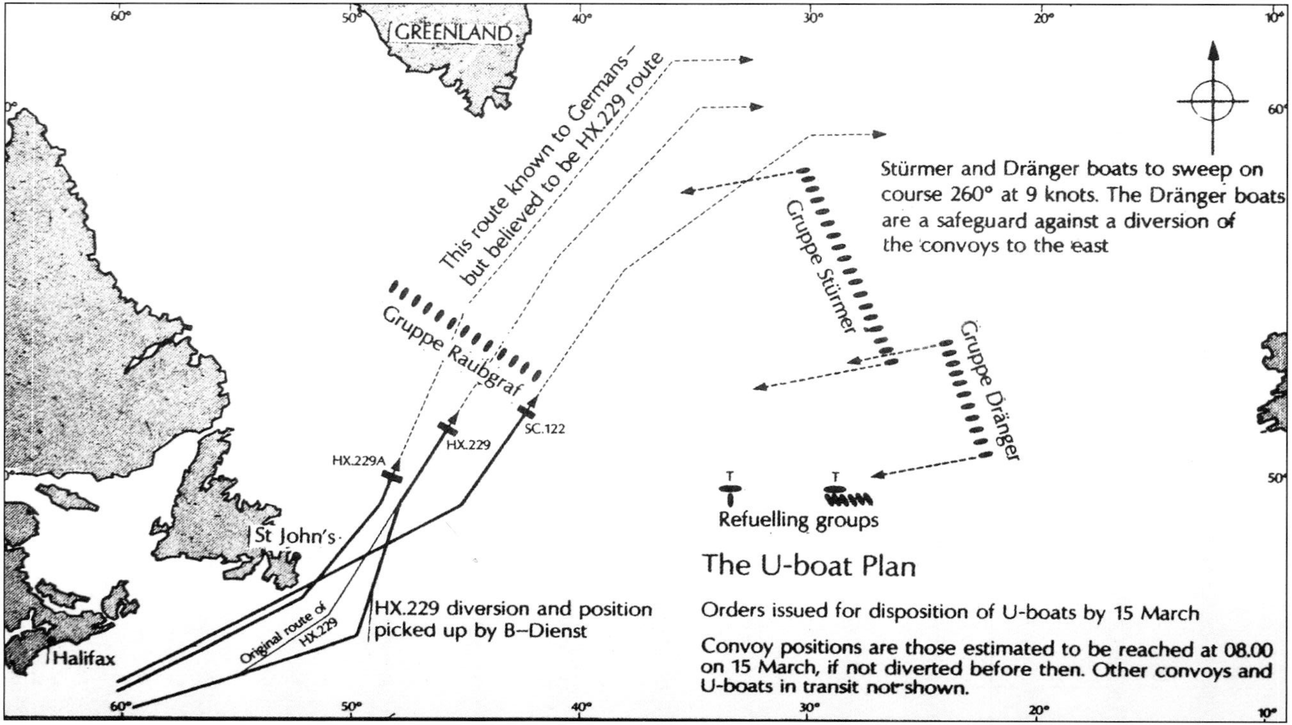

Stürmer and Dränger boats to sweep on
course 260° at 9 knots. The Dränger boats
are a safeguard against a diversion of
the convoys to the east

Gruppe Dränger

Gruppe Stürmer

Refuelling groups

The U-boat Plan

Orders issued for disposition of U-boats by 15 March

Convoy positions are those estimated to be reached at 08.00
on 15 March, if not diverted before then. Other convoys and
U-boats in transit not shown.

This route known to Germans –
but believed to be HX.229 route

Gruppe Raubgraf

GREENLAND

SC.122

HX.229

HX.229A

HX.229 diversion and position
picked up by B–Dienst

St John's

Original route of
HX.229

Halifax

38

CHART 8

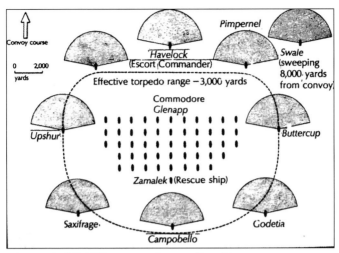

Diagram 1. SC. 122's escort and covoy disposition

The intention is to prevent a U-boat from getting within effective torpedo range of the ships. The shaded cone ahead of each escort is the area covered by its Asdic. Most escorts also had radar with a range of 4,000 yards, sufficient to provide a complete radar-covered zone around a well escorted convoy, but a surfaced U-boat at night was not easy to detect with radar. Escort screens could be altered at any time and, at night, the escort commander often took up a new position behind the convoy in action. *(Wireman R.A. White, H.M.S. Pennywort)*

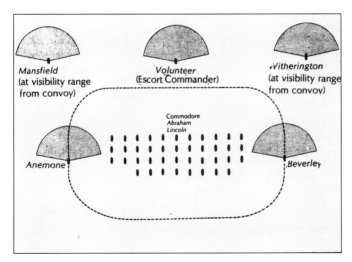

Diagram 2. HX.229's escort and covoy disposition

CHART 9

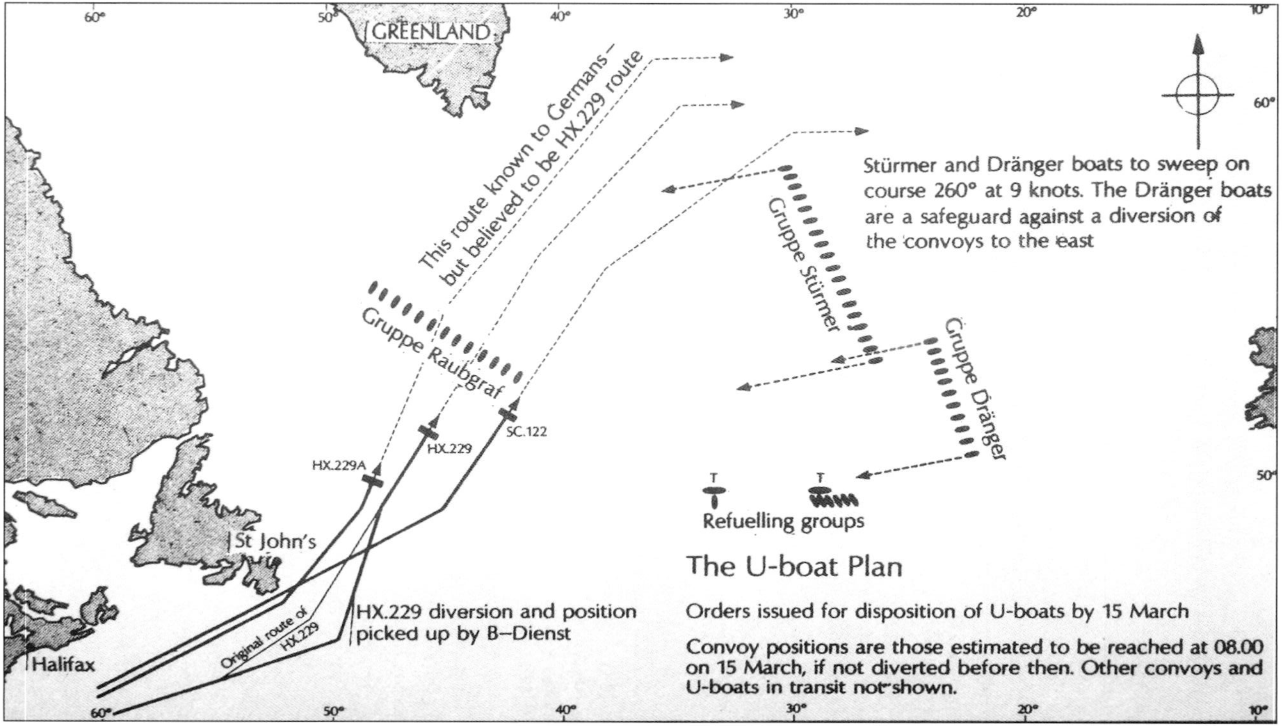

Stürmer and Dränger boats to sweep on course 260° at 9 knots. The Dränger boats are a safeguard against a diversion of the convoys to the east

Gruppe Dränger

Gruppe Stürmer

Refuelling groups

The U-boat Plan

Orders issued for disposition of U-boats by 15 March

Convoy positions are those estimated to be reached at 08.00 on 15 March, if not diverted before then. Other convoys and U-boats in transit not shown.

This route known to Germans – but believed to be HX.229 route

Gruppe Raubgraf

GREENLAND

SC.122

HX.229

HX.229A

HX.229 diversion and position picked up by B-Dienst

Original route of HX.229

St John's

Halifax

CHART 10

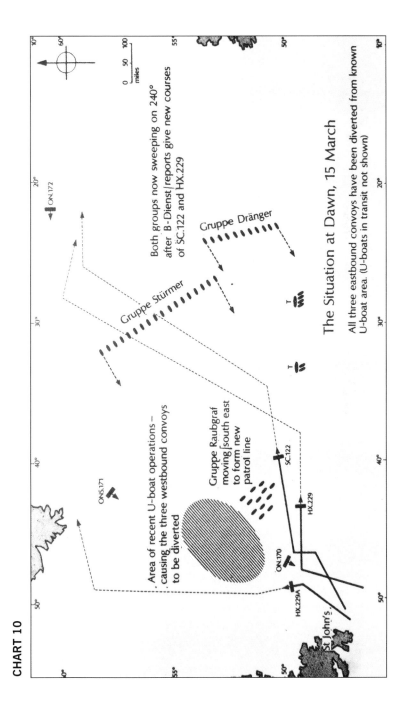

ON.172

ON.171

ONS.171

St John's

HX.229A

ON.170

HX.229

SC.122

Gruppe Raubgraf moving south east to form new patrol line

Area of recent U-boat operations – causing the three westbound convoys to be diverted

Gruppe Stürmer

Gruppe Dränger

Both groups now sweeping on 240° after B-Dienst reports give new courses of SC.122 and HX.229

0   50   100
         miles

The Situation at Dawn, 15 March

All three eastbound convoys have been diverted from known U-boat area. (U-boats in transit not shown)

41

CHART 11

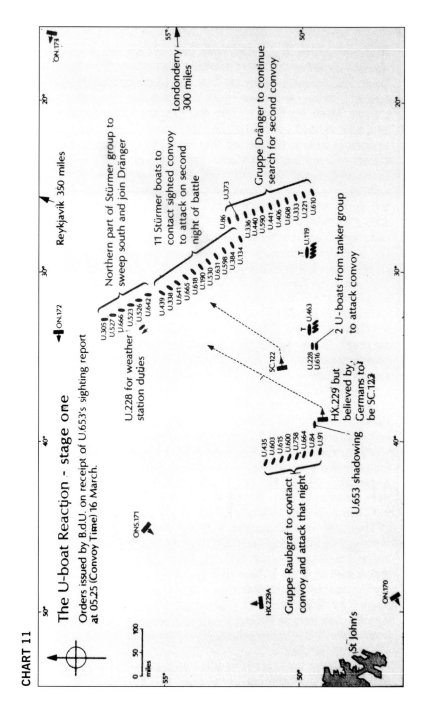

The U-boat Reaction - stage one

Orders issued by B.d.U. on receipt of U.653's sighting report at 05.25 (Convoy Time) 16 March.

Reykjavik 350 miles

Londonderry 300 miles

Northern part of Stürmer group to sweep south and join Dränger

11 Stürmer boats to contact convoy to attack on second night of battle

Gruppe Dränger to continue search for second convoy

U.228 for weather station duties

2 U-boats from tanker group to attack convoy

HX.229 but believed by Germans to be SC.122

U.653 shadowing

Gruppe Raubgraf to contact convoy and attack that night

St John's

ON.170

ON.171

ONS.171

HX229A

ONS.172

ON.173

SC.122

U.305
U.527
U.666
U.523
U.526
U.642

U.439
U.338
U.641
U.665
U.618
U.530
U.190
U.631
U.598
U.384
U.134

U.86
U.373
U.336
U.440
U.590
U.441
U.406
U.608
U.333
U.221
U.610

U.119

U.463
U.228
U.616

U.435
U.603
U.615
U.600
U.758
U.664
U.84
U.91

0   50   100
miles

42

CHART 12

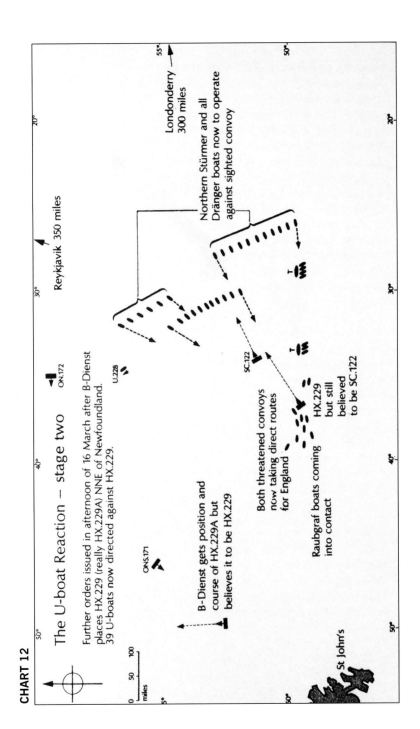

The U-boat Reaction – stage two

Further orders issued in afternoon of 16 March after B-Dienst places HX.229 (really HX.229A) NNE of Newfoundland. 39 U-boats now directed against HX.229.

Reykjavik 350 miles

Londonderry 300 miles

Northern Stürmer and all Dränger boats now to operate against sighted convoy

ON.172

U.228

ONS.171

B-Dienst gets position and course of HX.229A but believes it to be HX.229

Both threatened convoys now taking direct routes for England

SC.122

HX.229 but still believed to be SC.122

Raubgraf boats coming into contact

St John's

50° 40° 30° 20°

55°

50°

miles
0   50   100

CHART 13

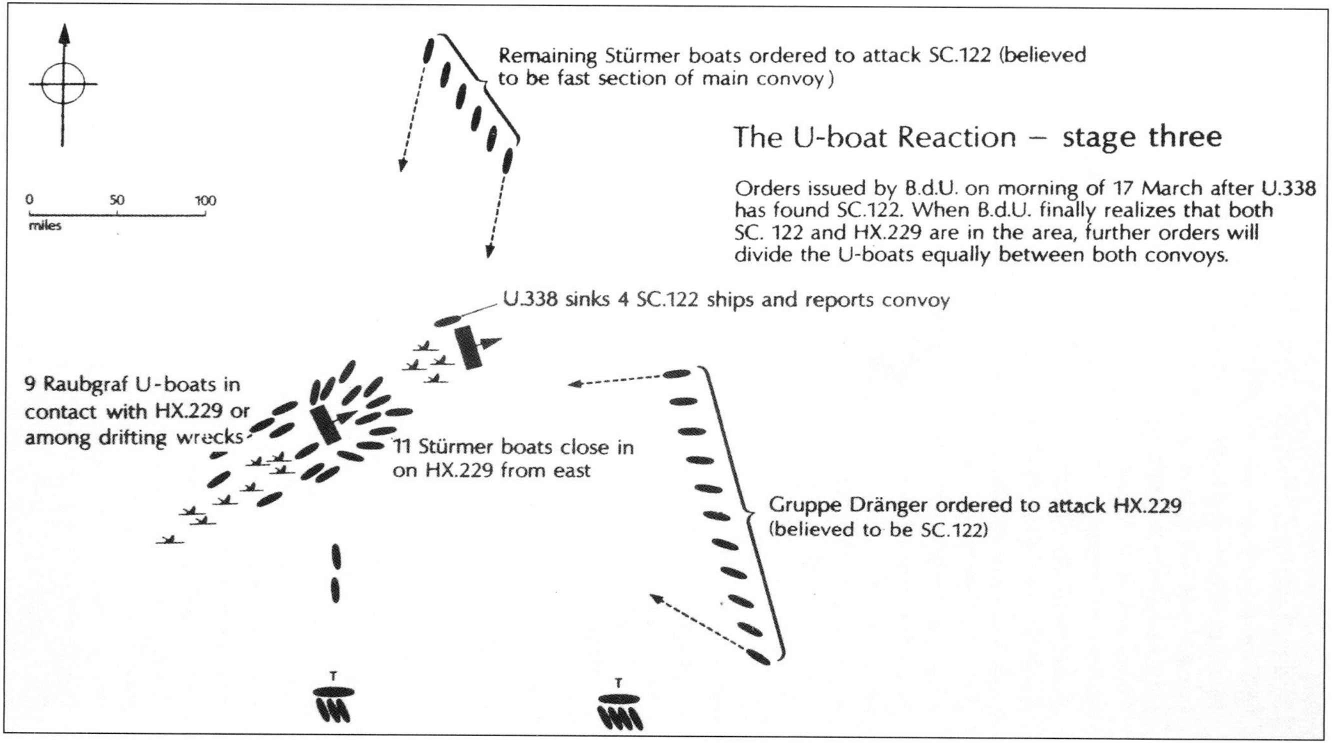

The U-boat Reaction – stage three

Orders issued by B.d.U. on morning of 17 March after U.338 has found SC.122. When B.d.U. finally realizes that both SC. 122 and HX.229 are in the area, further orders will divide the U-boats equally between both convoys.

Remaining Stürmer boats ordered to attack SC.122 (believed to be fast section of main convoy)

U.338 sinks 4 SC.122 ships and reports convoy

Gruppe Dränger ordered to attack HX.229 (believed to be SC.122)

'11 Stürmer boats close in on HX.229 from east

9 Raubgraf U-boats in contact with HX.229 or among drifting wrecks

0   50   100
miles

CHART 14

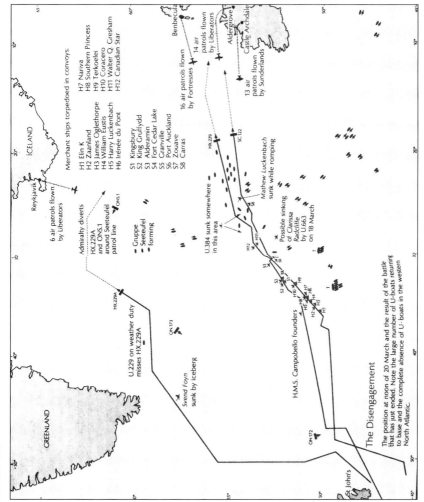

GREENLAND

ICELAND

Reykjavik

6 air patrols flown
by Liberators

Merchant ships torpedoed in convoys:

H1 Elin K
H2 Zaanland
H3 James Oglethorpe
H4 William Eustis
H5 Harry Luckenbach
H6 Irénée du Pont

H7 Nariva
H8 Southern Princess
H9 Terkoelei
H10 Coracero
H11 Walter Q. Gresham
H12 Canadian Star

S1 Kingsbury
S2 King Gruffydd
S3 Alderamin
S4 Fort Cedar Lake
S5 Granville
S6 Port Auckland
S7 Zouave
S8 Carras

Admiralty diverts
HX229A
and ONS1
around Seeteufel
patrol line

Gruppe
Seeteufel
forming

ONS1

HX229A

U.229 on weather duty
misses HX229A

ON172

Svend Foyn
sunk by iceberg

H.M.S. Campobello founders

ON172

St. John's

U.384 sunk
somewhere
in this area

Mathew Luckenbach
sunk while romping

Possible sinking
of Clarissa
Radcliffe
by U663
on 18 March

HX229

SC122

16 air patrols flown
by Fortresses

14 air
patrols flown
by Liberators

13 air
patrols flown
by Sunderlands

Benbecula

Aldergrove

Castle Archdale

The Disengagement

The position at noon of 20 March and the result of the battle
that has just ended. Note the large number of U-boats returning
to base and the complete absence of U-boats in the western
North Atlantic.

45

CHART 15

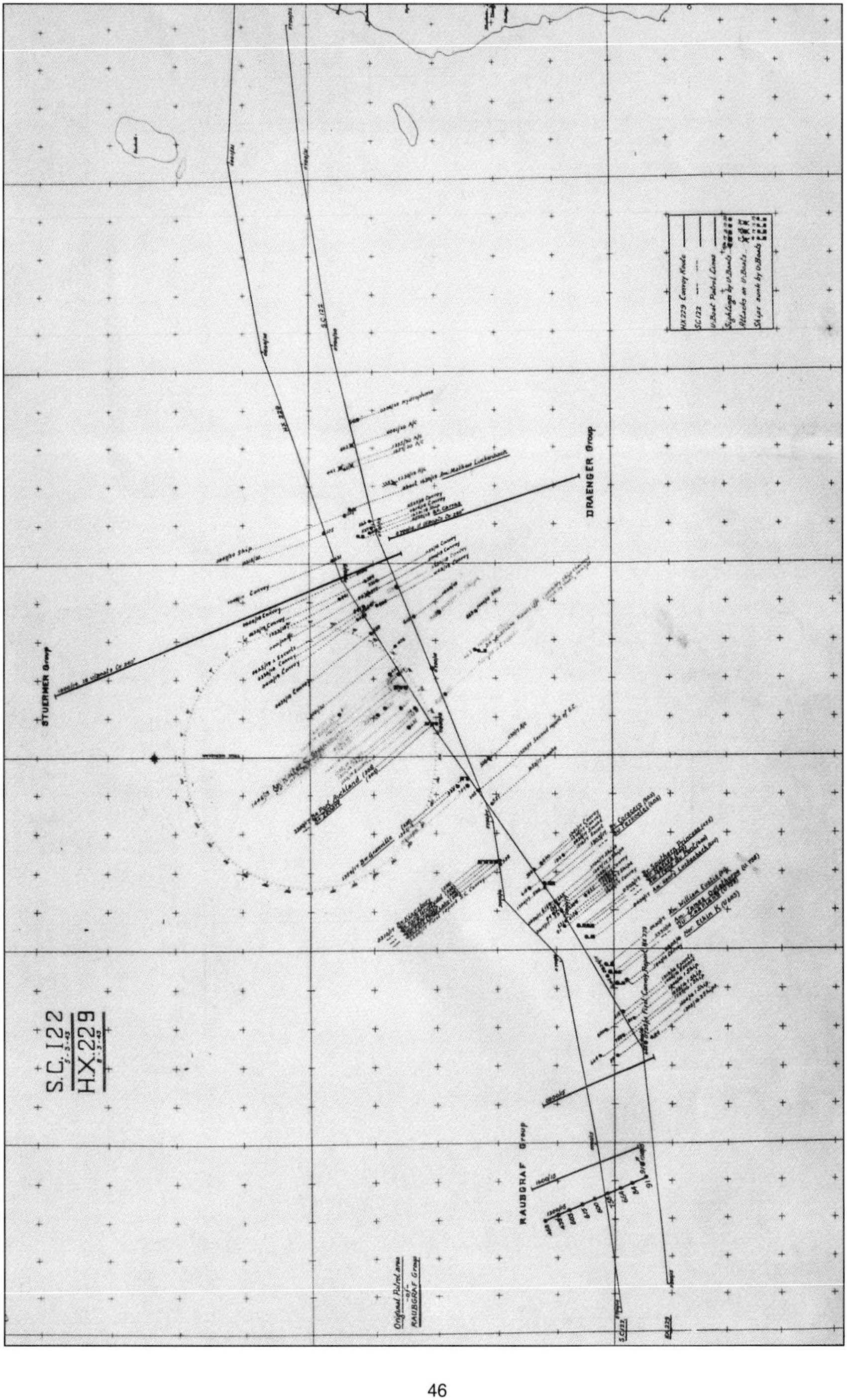

S.C.122
5-3-43
HX.229
8-3-43
STUERMER Group
DRAENGER Group
RAUBGRAF Group
Original Patrol area of RAUBGRAF Group
HX229 Convoy Route
SC122
U-Boat Patrol Lines
Sightings by U-Boats
Attacks on U-Boats
Ships sunk by U-Boats

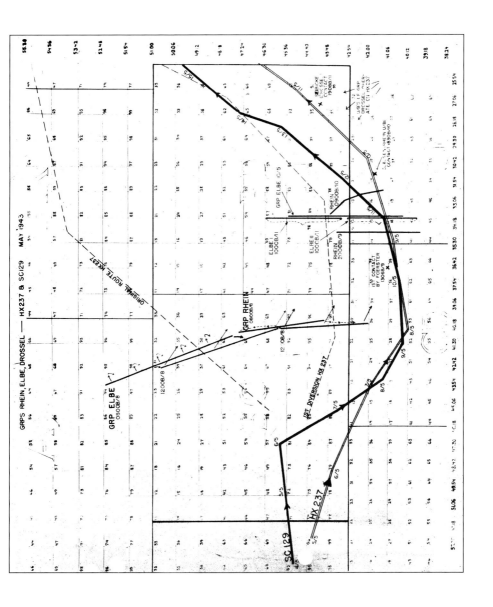

GRPS RHEIN, ELBE, DROSSEL — HX237 & SC129   MAY 1943

47

HU 631140 - The capture of the German submarine U-110 by HMS Bulldog, 10th May 1941. A party from HMS Bulldog prepares to board the submarine.